CW0063440B

❧ ALICE ❧

ROSE K. HUGHES

ALICE

Copyright © Rose K. Hughes 1993

ISBN 1 85863 097 5

First Published 1993 by
MINERVA PRESS
315–317 Regent Street
London W1R 7YB

Printed in Great Britain

⊰ ALICE ⊱

Rose K. Hughes

The women of today are very fortunate.

There is help available if faced with situations such as
the lady in this story suffered.
Grief - Poverty - Degradation - Humiliation & Abuse.

Surviving only by her strength of character and sheer
guts.

**This is the story
of
∞ ALICE ∞**

ෆ ALICE ෨

•PREFACE•

Monday morning in Lambeth Road was bustling with women and girls in coarse aprons. These were made from sacks opened at the seams and fastened around their waists with tape or string. All going in one direction to the washhouse, where for a few pence one could get hot water and the use of a copper and mangle for an allotted time. This service was widely used by families living in the area, as most houses only had a cold tap or pump in the back-yard.

Alice Swanson joined this band most Monday mornings with her family's dirty washing, having left school at thirteen, she was given many menial tasks by her mother Susannah Swanson.

Being the eldest girl at home much was expected of her. She adored Andy her brother who was eleven, hated her ten year old sister Ellen, known as Nell, because she was Mum's favourite and could do no wrong. She also had an elder sister Rose who did not live at home. Alice often visited her in Pimlico where she was in service. She admired Rose in her smart uniform and vowed as soon as she was old enough she would follow in her footsteps. After all she thought I might as well be a drudge and get paid for it, as this is all she was at home and rarely got a kind word.

Billy was her youngest brother, and the main reason why Susannah Swanson was so indifferent to Alice. Six years earlier, whilst minding Billy aged two, she had let him fall off a table, thus resulting in a fracture to his right leg. This leg withered and Billy was left with one leg shorter than the other. He had to wear a surgical boot with several inches of wooden sole to keep him level. Doctors disagreed with Susannah Swanson that this condition was a result of the fracture, but she would accept no other explanation.

Alice loved her brother, and always felt responsible for his limp. Her father, Andrew Matthew Swanson was a quiet kindly man, very much under the thumb of his bossy wife. He was a painter and paper-hanger by trade and had little to say in his family affairs.

❡ Chapter 1 ❡

It was a cold January morning when the news broke that the Queen was dead. Victoria's 60 years of reign had ended.

Alice felt very sad, after all, she was named after the Queen's second daughter Princess Alice. But this day, the 22nd January 1901, would be a day Alice would never forget, for more than one reason.

Mrs Swanson was busy chatting with her neighbours at the front gate, all voicing their sadness at the loss of the dear Queen. Alice saw her chance to slip away for awhile.

Through the back-yard and over the wall she hurried, making her way to the arches in Westminster Bridge Road where her friend Teddy was mucking out his uncle's stables. Seeing her approach he called, "Come on Alice give us a hand."

This she promptly did, picking up a shovel she helped him pile the stenching straw into a large bin outside, (to be picked up and used as fertiliser), Teddy was paid tuppence for the job.

"What are you going to do with that?" asked Alice, fully expecting to receive a half, Teddy ignored her question and just said, "Come on."

Alice had to run to keep up with him. They crossed the road that led into the Lower Marsh, a market packed with stalls and barrows. He stopped at one laden with all kinds of bottles, sorting amongst these he picked up a small phial of ink.

"How much?" he asked.

"One penny," was the reply.

"I'll have it," he said, "also a nib."

Paying for his purchases he took Alice's arm and said,

"Lets go."

Alice was mystified as to why he wanted these items, but Teddy kept his reasons to himself.

Realising she had been away for two hours Alice called out, "I have got to go, see you later," and she ran home.

Mrs Swanson had now become aware that Alice was missing, and wondered how she had left the house without being seen, glad to get her sister into trouble Nell said, "She probably climbed the back wall." So seating herself at the back kitchen window Susannah Swanson awaited Alice's return.

After a while a leg appeared over the wall, followed by the body of Alice.

"Don't try to hide, come in here!" she heard. Going into the kitchen she was greeted with a brutal smack to her face.

"Where have you been?" screamed her mother. Alice had her answer ready, having decided to tell a lie if she got caught.

"I have been to church to pray for the Queen."

Mrs Swanson was taken aback by this reply, and being a catholic felt maybe she had been too harsh with the girl.

"Go and wash your face" she said, "I'll make a cup of tea," adding "But in future ask if you want to go out."

Alice, still crying, vowed that she would leave home as soon as she could.

Later that day Mrs Swanson, feeling guilty at the sight of Alice's swollen face said, "You can go out if you want to but be back before it gets dark." Alice needed no second telling and took off as fast as her legs could carry her. She made her way to the Canterbury Arches to the den where Teddy and the gang always met.

"What's happened?" they asked seeing Alice's marked face

"My mum hit me," she said bursting into tears. She received hugs and kisses from them all in sympathy, so felt life wasn't so bad after all.

Teddy pushing a wooden box towards her, said "Sit down I'll do you first."

"Do what?" said Alice.

"You'll see, hold out your hand."

This Alice did and Teddy proceeded to draw a ring in ink on her third finger left hand. Alice was ecstatic and wished it was a real one, but yelled when he started pricking her finger with the needle and applying more ink.

She screeched, "What are you doing?"

"It's called a tattoo," said Teddy and began explaining that they all had one. She calmed down as Teddy said, "Look Mary has one on her arm."

Not to be outdone Alice decided to have Teddy's name on hers. By now he was getting to be an expert and swiftly drew his name on her forearm, pricking the letters one by one and applying more Indian ink.

It was a painful procedure,

"How long will it last?" asked Alice.

"Forever and ever," he replied.

She went home a much happier person, quite pleased with her newly acquired work of art. But alas! Next morning, on waking realised her arm ached and was horrified to see a red and angry mass where Teddy had written his name. Also, the third finger on her left hand was very swollen.

"Oh God, what can I do?" she moaned.

Finding a clean rag she wound it around her arm and finger, praying her mother would not see it.

But the eagle eye of Susannah Swanson soon noticed the bandaged finger and said, "What's wrong?"

"Not much," said Alice, "I grazed it getting over the wall."
"Serves you right, that's your punishment," she replied, and taking Alice's hand unwound the rag.

"What on earth!" she exclaimed and appeared quite concerned seeing the angry festering finger. "Hospital for you my girl" she said.

"Oh no!" yelled Alice. She was terrified of doctors and always ran past St Thomas's Hospital, not bearing to look at it. Mary Hanigan had told her that's where you go to die. Alice was petrified at the thought of death.

When she was ten years old she was taken to see her Godmother Bessie Purchace in her coffin. The cold waxen face still haunted her. In floods of tears she confessed the whole story. She was promptly marched off to the dreaded hospital. Arriving at the Out-patients Department, she was asked by the sister in charge the reason for their visit. Mrs Swanson explained why they had come. They were instructed to sit on a wooden bench along the corridor. Everywhere was so clean and smelt strongly of carbolic.

Half an hour later Alice's name was called. She was terrified and clung to her mother.

The sister said, "Alright you may go with her."

Seated at a table in a white coat was a very stern looking man. The nurse removed the bandages from Alice's finger and arm for the Doctor to examine.

He looked at her inquiringly, "Who did this?" he asked in a very demanding voice. But Alice would not tell on her dear Teddy and did not utter a sound.

Losing patience he instructed the nurse about the treatment, and waved his arm in dismissal.

Whilst Alice was having her dressings applied, Mrs Swanson was directed to the Almoners Office. This was routine - where one was given a means test to determine whether they could afford to pay something towards the treatment received. It was decided that she could pay a small donation, two pence in the box she was told, this she did with great reluctance.

Poor Alice appeared, accompanied by a nurse and joined her mother looking a very sorry sight indeed.

Arriving home Mrs Swanson soon related the story to the family. Alice sat silently, wishing she had never seen Teddy or his rotten ink.

Andy put his arm around her and said, "Don't worry Sis, it will soon get better."

Nell looking scornful, said she must be mad and would probably end up in Bedlam - Bethlem Institution for the Insane, which was a stones throw from Morton place in Lambeth Road

- where in the dead of night one could hear the cries of its poor demented inmates.

One day Alice and her friends feeling bored and seeking excitement climbed over the wall of this place and peeping through a barred window, saw crouched in a corner on a bed of straw a figure so grotesque, snarling and spitting, with nails like talons. They ran as fast as their legs would carry them away from that horrible sight.

Mrs Swanson seeing the distress on Alice's face said, "That's enough Nell," and putting her arms around her poor misguided daughter made her promise never to meet any of her friends, or go to the Den again. To which she readily agreed, after all the suffering she had endured. She never wanted to hear the name Teddy again, little realising that his name was written forever on her arm.

The next six months were uneventful. Alice continued her daily grind, helping to keep the little house in Morton Place spic and span, with its windows gleaming, starched white lace curtains, shining brass knocker and letter-box, and white earth-stoned front door step. It stood out amongst the dinginess of its neighbours.

Mrs Swanson was a very proud person, quite a snob in her own way. She wished Alice was more like her sister Nell, who appeared very gentle and ladylike.

But Nell was only required to do the dusting and very light chores, so compared with Alice's daily routine she had a very easy life.

ℂ **Chapter 2** ℬ

It was August 9th, 1902, not only was it Alice's fourteenth birthday but Edward VII was being crowned at Westminster Abbey. His official Coronation had been arranged for June 26th, but unfortunately was cancelled due to his illness. There was much celebration, especially in Morton Place where all the residents contributed towards a street party. Most of the adults got drunk. Children ran wild and gorged themselves on cakes and jelly. Alice danced with gusto to the barrel-organ and declared, "this is truly the best day of my life!"

Susannah Swanson's friend Mrs Holt was housekeeper to the Honourable Mrs Selworthy, a widow of some renown, at her large house in Vincent Square. She managed to obtain a position of kitchen maid for Alice, who was delighted to learn she could now leave home. So two days later with her clothes packed in a large straw bag, she said good-bye to her beloved Andy and Billy and even kissed her sister Nell, hugged her mother and father promising to be a 'good girl' and made her way to Vincent Square.

Arriving at the large five storey house, she suddenly panicked and wished she had let Andy come with her as he had wanted to. So going down the stone steps that led to the basement she knocked at the kitchen door.

It was answered by a stout pleasant looking lady who said, "Hallo, you must be Alice. Come in and take your coat off, I'll make you a cup of tea. My name is Mrs Wilson and I am the cook in charge."

After meeting this kind, cheery lady Alice soon forgot her fears.

"Do your best, work well and don't slack," she advised, "and you will have no problems here. Come, I'll show you to your quarters."

Up many stairs to the top of the house they went. The room was just big enough for a single bed, a small chest of drawers and a wash-stand with a jug and basin. The stark white walls were bare except for a black crucifix. Alice was disappointed, but glad to have a room of her own. Two bells hung on the wall over the bed, she soon learnt only too well why they were there. Hardly had she unpacked when one of them rang summoning her to the kitchen.

Mrs Wilson handed her a linen bag and said, "Here is your uniform, change quickly and come back down." Alice went up the stairs two at a time and eagerly undid the string, but found not a navy and white uniform like Rose's but a drab brown calico dress with a large beige twill apron and cap, one thing she was thankful for was that it had long sleeves and would hide her shameful tattoo, the ring was not so noticeable.

She joined Mrs Wilson who ran an approving eye over her then said, "Come along, I'll take you to meet Madam."

Going not via the dingy back stairs the staff used, but through the splendid front hall with its marble tiles and gold framed mirrors, up two flights of Persian carpeted stairs to Madam's sitting room. Alice's eyes feasted on the magnificent furniture and drapes. She had never seen such splendour, but no word of welcome greeted her, just a curt, "Good Morning!"

"I expect very loyal service from you Alice. If you do as you are told and work hard you will be very happy here, I will give you one months trial."

"Yes Madam" said Alice "Thank you," then being nudged by the cook curtsied and left the room. So began the life in service she had so looked forward to.

For the first time in her fourteen years Alice was grateful to her mother. She had taught her well, so the work required of her was not too difficult. Lighting fires and stoves at five o'clock in the morning, black leading grates, cleaning the brass and silver, filling huge kettles and pans to supply hot water for the upstairs rooms. Peeling potatoes, shelling peas, scraping carrots, parsnips and swedes, or whatever the cook needed for the menu. Alice was sure the amount of food prepared in the household would feed an army.

She did not often see any of the Honourables other than Madam, who made a daily visit to the kitchen. Sometimes she would see them getting into their carriages from her tiny bedroom window.

On her half day off she went back to Morton Place to see her family where surprisingly, she was made very welcome. Her mother having realised Alice's worth, tried to make up for her past in considerations. She also became aware that her daughter was becoming a striking looking girl, with her black hair and dark brown eyes, she appeared almost Italian. Susannah Swanson always said her grandmother came from Italy - no one really knew whether this was true or not.

As time went by life became easier for Alice. She progressed to working upstairs under Mrs Bolt, the housekeeper. Her duties were mainly the bedrooms, dressing rooms and closets, also laundering the fine clothes of her employer. Mrs Bolt appreciated Alice's efforts and rewarded her with some of the young ladies discarded clothing.

She was also given a bedroom on the fourth floor, which not only had a wooden bedstead, but an alcove where she could hang her newly acquired wardrobe.

Now seventeen years old and having the status of being an upstairs maid she was entitled to one whole day per week off. It was on one of these days that Alice met George Brown. Her sister Rose who was now nineteen years old, took her to see the famous artist Violet Lorraine at the Canterbury Music Hall.

Just as they were leaving after the show, Rose said, "Hold on a minute, there's someone I want you to meet" and turning to a tall good looking young man of about 18 years of age said; "George, this is my younger sister, Alice."

Alice was in heaven when he asked to walk her home. So with Rose's request for him to take good care of her little sister, 'or else!' he accompanied her to Vincent Square.

George told her he worked in Covent Garden as a cartminder. Alice had no idea what this was, so he explained that his job was a very hard one (as later in life she was to find out). George lived in Vauxhall Bridge Road with his mother, his father having died some years earlier. His mother was well known in the vicinity as a mean and contemptuous woman. She was a money-lender and charged very high interest rates, so the poor wretches who were unfortunate enough to borrow from her, were rarely out of debt. George was not proud of this, but after walking out with Alice for some months decided to take her home to meet his mother.

They disliked each other instantly. The visit was not a success, so on her next day off she took George to Morton Place to meet her family. With much pride she introduced him. Her mother supplied an excellent tea, served with the best Doulton china. This, thought Alice, was indeed an honour.

Alice compared her mother to Mary Brown and decided most definitely who was the best. She felt sorry not to have loved her mother more, and gave her a big kiss and hug when they were leaving, promising to come again soon.

Life indeed was very happy for Alice and more so on her next day off. Deciding to surprise George, she took a walk along Millbank passing the Houses of Parliament, through Whitehall to Trafalgar Square, crossing into William IV Street and approached Maiden Lane.

She saw George looking very important, giving a porter with a heavily laden barrow instructions on where to unload. She watched him count the sacks of potatoes as the porter transferred them from his barrow to a horse and cart belonging to H.C.Walton.

Turning, he saw her and came quickly to her side. Kissing her on the cheek and putting his arm around her waist he said, "Come and sit on this box, I'll soon be finished." The box was his office, his right of pitch, his domain.

At 11.30 am when the market was quiet, and most of the customers had left, George decided to leave also, having been there since the early hour of 3.30 am.

He guided Alice across the narrow lane, through a wrought-iron gate, down a flight of steps into Corpus Christi the Catholic Church. Alice thought it was the sweetest little church that she had ever seen. Holding her hand he took her down the aisle to the front pew. There he confirmed his love for her and asked her to marry him, Alice nodded unable to speak. She fell to her knees and thanked God for giving her George. They left the church full of happiness and love.

The next day, Alice broke the news of her impending marriage to Mrs Bolt, not getting the congratulations that she had expected. "But, oh dear, you will have to leave." She explained that married women were not employed in service unless the husband held a position in the same household.

In her excitement Alice had not given this much thought.

"Don't say anything yet," warned Mrs Bolt, hoping that maybe the marriage was a long way off or perhaps would not even take place. With Alice being such a good worker, she did not want to lose her, but Alice's head was only filled with thoughts of George and that on her next day off they were going to buy an engagement ring. Never did a week go so slowly, but eventually the day came.

She met George at Victoria and they walked to Strutton Ground. They gazed in many jewellers shops, then Alice saw a gold band with two small hearts entwined. It was priced at six shillings.

"Oh how lovely!" she exclaimed, "But it is a lot of money."

"Come on, let's go in and try it on," said George.

The jewellers assistant got the ring from the window and assured them what a bargain it was, being an unredeemed pledge, which is an article pawned for a sum of money but never collected. George slipped the ring on Alice's finger, it fitted perfectly. Thank God, thought Alice, it covers the tormenting tattoo completely. Informing the assistant that his fiancée would keep the ring on, he paid the sum of six shillings, and obtained a receipt. Now instead of hiding her left hand as she had done for many years, Alice walked with her hand proudly across her chest, the other holding George's arm for all the world to see.

George decided on a little celebration and took her to the "Windsor Castle" pub near Victoria Station. On arriving they were greeted warmly. Alice was surprised how well known George was. He proudly introduced her as his bride to be. Everyone clapped and offered their congratulations.

They asked, "What would you like to drink?"

Alice, not ever having been asked this before hesitated, then remembering the cook's favourite tipple, answered, "Port and Lemon please."

There were three on the table before she had time to drink one. George joined his friends in a game of cards. Alice was happy in her new surroundings. She observed that most of George's friends appeared to be Irish.

Later on, seeing Alice's face becoming flushed, George decided it was time to leave. After saying their 'good-byes' George said, "We'll walk to the park," crossing Buckingham Palace Road, passing the Palace and into Green Park, where on a wooden bench they planned their future life together and decided on a Christmas wedding.

It was nearly 9 o'clock, so they slowly walked back to Vincent Square, as Alice had to be in by 10 o'clock. They said goodnight, Alice giving George a long lingering kiss. She was eager to show off her ring, so instead of going to her room she went down to the kitchen where the staff were having a cup of cocoa after a long evenings work. They all wished her luck and admired the ring; so taking a drink with her she went to her room.

She could not sleep and kept lighting the candle to gaze at her new ring, thankful that it hid the shameful mark. Suddenly realising that George knew nothing of the other one on her arm as she always wore long sleeves, and thinking when they were married he would see her bare arms.

She decided to tell him when next they met. Just then a terrible thought crossed her mind. Supposing he got upset and didn't want to marry her, having another man's name on her arm. Wishing she had told him when he asked about the ring tattoo on her finger, she cried herself to sleep.

The news of her engagement travelled through the house. Madam sent instructions for Alice to be in the Drawing-Room at 11 o'clock. The night of misery had taken its toll, her poor face pale, with red rimmed eyes, was quickly noticed by Madam.

"What's wrong?" she asked, "You do not appear to be a happy, blushing bride to be."

Alice unable to contain herself burst into tears. Ringing for Mrs Bolt, Madam bid Alice, "Go to your room."

Mrs Bolt was asked if she knew why Alice was so distressed. Answering that she had no idea, was told to find out. Madam had jumped to the conclusion that the girl was pregnant. Mrs Bolt was quick to come to Alice's defence and said she was sure this was not the case. Alice was a nice God fearing girl, and came from a good home, to which she was well aquainted with, Mrs Swanson being her best friend.

Going to Alice's room she found a more composed person who readily gave the reason for her behaviour. She told Mrs Bolt about her fears of losing George and about the tattoo.

"Poor little soul, if he loves you that won't make any difference" she assured Alice, "Come down and have a nice cup of tea, then get on with the beds. In the meantime I will explain your problem to Madam, who will be very relieved that things were not so bad after all."

It was a very subdued Alice that met George on Saturday. Looking at her he remarked, "You're very quiet tonight, anything wrong?"

She did not answer him but rolled up her sleeve saying, "I'm sorry, but I was only thirteen." He stared at her arm then at her face for a few seconds, then roaring with laughter unbuttoned his shirt to reveal a heart with G & M across his chest, saying he had done this when he was sixteen. They fell into each others arms, Alice crying, George laughing. The torment was over.

They then went to Morton Place to tell of their engagement and intended marriage. Susannah Swanson was genuinely pleased, she liked George.

"Go up and tell your Dad," she said, "He is upstairs in bed."

She told Alice that he had been poorly for a few weeks. "The Doctor said it's caused by the paint fumes..."

Alice did not wait to hear anymore, but hurried up to the bedroom. She was shocked to see how ill her father looked,

"Oh Dad" she cried, "Why didn't they let me know?"

"I'm alright love" he said, "Don't you worry." But as she showed him her ring he had a fit of coughing and fell back exhausted. She kissed him and said she would come and see him again soon. He nodded with a smile.

This was the last time she saw her father - he died that night. The funeral was a lavish affair; Mrs Swanson did her husband proud. The hearse was drawn by four black horses with purple plumes; two carriages followed with drawn black curtains at the windows. The coffin was oak with brass handles and a six foot cross of flowers adorned the lid. The neighbours sent the customary wreath, a 'Gates of Heaven.'

Alice laid a single red rose on the coffin, obtained from the gardener at Vincent Square, one of Madam's prize blooms, no less from her greenhouse. She would not go to see her father in his coffin, she wanted to remember him alive, not a white and waxen image like her godmother.

⊰ Chapter 3 ⊱

Due to her father's passing, Alice could no longer have the big white wedding they had planned, so she decided on a quiet Wednesday afternoon service, arranged with father Gilliard at St.George's Cathedral.

Alice wore a grey suit, a smart tricorn velvet hat to match and patent kid ankle boots. She looked absolutely beautiful. Even Susannah Swanson had to admit her daughter was a sight for sore eyes.

Mary Brown arrived in her best black, looking more as if she were attending a funeral than a wedding. But nothing could daunt Alice today. She knew her future mother-in-law's feelings towards her were not genial, but resolved that when she was married to George she would try to improve their relationship.

George was at the church, accompanied by his best man Michael Murphy. He handed Alice a spray of orchids. She was indeed in heaven, and so they were married. Everything was perfect. Mrs Swanson arranged the reception at Morton Place, just a quiet affair. There was plenty of food and drink and surprisingly she got on quite well with Mary Brown. They both tucked into the gin bottle. This amused Alice and George who decided to leave them to it and go home to the two rooms on the fourth floor of his mother's house in Bessborough

Gardens. They had rented these from her for five shillings a week. It was not very well furnished but Alice soon made it comfortable.

She was allowed to carry on working at Vincent Square, but was now non-resident, having the afternoons off and working a split duty, mornings and evenings. Life was all so wonderful and George proved to be a very good husband. Alice indeed counted her blessings and it was no surprise that in two months she was pregnant. But it was not at all how she had thought it would be.

She felt absolutely terrible. The morning sickness made going to work very tiring, so George insisted that she gave in her notice. Madam was not very pleased at this, workers of Alice's calibre were very hard to come by, but she wished her well and gave her a box of baby clothes, which George promptly gave away, saying his child would not be wearing anybody's discarded clothing even if they were from the aristocracy.

Being at home all day left Alice feeling very bored, so she offered to help her mother-in-law in the house. Having six furnished bedsits on three floors, Mary Brown was glad of her help. George was kept busy in his spare time being the secretary of the Liberal Club he was always arranging functions or fund raising for some charity or other. He was a good man and Alice could not have been happier.

On October 6th, 1908 Alice gave birth to a lovely eight pound boy. She was attended by a midwife well known around Vauxhall, having delivered most children in that area for ten years. Everyone respected Nurse Wiggins and called on her for births or deaths. She was expert at both.

The baby was christened George Andrew Joseph after his father and two deceased grandfathers. He was dressed in the best that money could buy and according to his father was the most precious, beautiful baby in the world. Meanwhile Susannah Swanson had met William Spoor, an eligible bachelor. She was quite smitten and when he proposed she accepted and married him, and so moved from Morton Place to upper class Tooting.

William had been left the house in Trevelyn Road by his mother who had followed her husband to an early grave the previous year. He was a kind man, a landscape gardener by trade. He welcomed Susannah and her family into his home, giving her carte-blanche to change whatever she wanted to. He owned a car which Billy was allowed to drive. Wearing a surgical boot was no disadvantage to Billy and he was soon behind the wheel, driving his mother and sister around Tooting.

Andy was not so happy with the move, so decided to join the Merchant Navy. He disappeared from the bosom of his family for some years. Rose also cut herself away from them; the last they heard she was going to marry a widower and move to Australia.

Alice would visit her mother and family from time to time, but always liked to be home when George returned from work.

One thing Alice always found very puzzling about her husband was his obsession. He loved anything Irish. All his friends were Irish, and he would be moved to tears listening to an Irish singer. He promised her one day he would take her to this lovely country. She often wondered how he knew this was so, as he had never been there, but was glad to be included in his dreams of the Emerald Isle.

Baby George was now nearly two years old. Alice was again pregnant, six months to be exact. One morning George came home from the market very distressed. Michael Murphy, his dearest friend, had been knocked down by a runaway horse, the cart had fallen on him killing him instantly, leaving a wife and six children. Alice had never seen him so devastated. But being the good soul he was, George soon organised a benefit for Michael's family.

Alice learnt a lesson from this. The Irish surely helped one another. Times were hard and money was scarce yet they handed over money they could ill afford. George collected the princely sum of twenty eight pounds, which he put into an envelope with a list of all who had contributed, ready to give the widow on the day of the funeral.

The sad day arrived, George told Alice to get herself and little George ready, while he went down to saddle up the pony and trap he was borrowing from his mother to take them to Kensal Green Cemetery.

"I'll come back for you shortly," he said.

Half an hour passed and Alice thought surely he hasn't gone without us. Carrying the boy in her arms she went downstairs to the back of the house, reaching the stables she called, "Where are you George?"

Pushing open the half-closed door she saw a sight one would never wish to see. Her dearest George lying prone among the straw, the saddle still in his hand.

He was dead.

Screaming, "Help for God's sake, help me!" She ran into the road, people came from all directions. Someone tried to lead her away, a neighbour took the little boy from her and said "Come with me," but she refused pleading, "No, let me go to my darling George."

She went back into the stable and held him in her arms crying, "Oh God, how could you?" Over and over again.

Soon the police arrived and arranged for George to be taken to Rochester Row Mortuary, informing her that there would be an autopsy and inquest.

Mary Brown appeared disbelieving what she was told about her son. She fell prostrate across his body. Alice tried to comfort her, some friends helped her into the house. Soon two mortuary attendants arrived with the casket on wheels to collect George's body. They told Alice to follow, so she walked beside her dear George along Vauxhall Bridge Road, her hand never leaving the container in which her husband lay.

On arriving at the mortuary she sat alone, bewildered and heartbroken in the corridor of this formidable building. Holding her hands against the child inside her for comfort, thinking that this must be a nightmare, but when a man appeared and handed her George's best suit and boots saying, "Come tomorrow at 3 o'clock for the death certificate and results of the autopsy," she realised it was not a dream but harsh reality.

Walking home, as if in a trance, too numb to even think about her son, she entered the house which was full of Mrs Brown's huge family. She slipped unnoticed upstairs to the top floor that had been her heaven for nearly three years, collapsed onto the bed and gave vent to her suffering.

"Oh my God, what am I going to do?" she cried.

Still clutching George's clothing in her arms as she rocked to and fro. After a while she rose and hung up the suit, put the boots in the cupboard, and made her way to her neighbours to collect her small son.

"Stay here tonight," said the kindly woman, but Alice said she would rather not, but thanking her, picked up her sleeping child and carried him home. Unable to sleep, she lit the fire, boiled the kettle and made a pot of tea. This helped her to think more clearly about the future. Now she had not only her son to provide for, but also the child she was expecting.

Opening her purse she counted three shillings and sixpence. She reached up and put her hand into George's suit pocket, she took out his notebook, some letters regarding the club and his keys. Frantically she began searching for the envelope containing the twenty eight pounds belonging to Mrs Murphy, but it was not there. She had seen George put it in his pocket before he went down to the ill-fated stable. Searching the waistcoat and trousers, which only revealed ten shillings and fourpence, she was filled with disgust. What had happened to it?

Surely no-one could take from a dead man especially one as good as her dear George, but she consoled herself by thinking the mortuary people must have put it away for safekeeping, they would give it to her when she went to collect the certificate.

Eventually, she fell asleep exhausted in the chair. It was daylight when she awoke. After washing herself and Georgie, and giving him his breakfast, she went down to see her mother-in-law. It was plain to see that Mary Brown was so wrapped up in her own grief, she had none spare for her, so putting her son into his pram she made her way to Rochester Row.

On arriving at the mortuary she asked to see the person in charge. A very stout bewhiskered man appeared and enquired if he could help her. She explained about the missing envelope. His attitude changed and becoming quite angry he asked, "Are you accusing my staff of stealing?"

"Well" said Alice, "If it was not put away for safekeeping, what has happened to it?"

He assured her that his staff were of the highest integrity and that it was very dangerous to make an accusation without adequate proof and advised her to look elsewhere for the envelope.

She left and walked to Green Park and sat on the seat where she and her dear George had planned their life together. Now he was gone and she was left alone to care for their children.

Later that afternoon she was in possession of the death certificate. The cause was diagnosed as a massive heart attack. George was found to have a heart so large that the doctors performing the autopsy were amazed that he had lived so long.

Mary Brown took control of the funeral arrangements, Alice being in no position to do so, financially or otherwise. There was no benefit collected for her by George's friends. Alice was sure they thought that she had kept Mrs Murphy's envelope containing the money. But they arrived with lots of flowers and wreaths at the funeral. Never was there such a turn out.

Standing by the grave she was comforted by Father Brown. (No relation to the family.) He came from St Ann's Church at Vauxhall just across the river. It was a blessing that she met this man, her family had not come to the funeral, having gone on holiday to Canvey Island. Father Brown took her under his wing after observing the situation, and more than once in her lifetime Alice was to be grateful to this man for his help.

Because of her pregnancy she could not think about finding work. The porters at Covent Garden collected twenty pounds for George's widow and called to give it to her, with many messages of sympathy. For the first time since George's death she felt thankful for this help and comfort.

On hearing that Alice had received this, Mary Brown made it clear that she still expected the five shillings rent. She made no secret of the fact that she did not like her daughter-in-law and only tolerated her for the sake of her son, but now he was gone, thought it better that she should move elsewhere.

Alice's feelings got the better of her she threw five shillings on to the floor, calling Mary Brown a mean miserable cow, picked up little Georgie and ran upstairs. Next day she found a furnished room in Grosvenor Road for three shillings a week, loaded her belongings on to the pram and left Bessborough Gardens.

Her money soon began to dwindle, she swallowed her pride and asked for some help from the Public Assistance, or as it was commonly known the Parish. But apart from some food tickets there wasn't much to be had.

One month after George's death, Alice woke up aware of a deep pain, she could hardly move, feeling faint she managed to crawl to the door. Calling loudly to her landlady Mrs Connell who helped her back to bed, she asked "Is it the baby?"

Alice said, "No, I am only seven months pregnant."

So the Doctor was quickly sent for. But, by the time he had arrived Alice had delivered, with Mrs Connell's help, a baby girl so tiny they could not believe she was alive. Quickly examining Alice, and stating that he would send in a nurse, he wrapped the baby in a clean towel and took her to Westminster

Hospital. For a whole week Alice never even knew whether her baby was dead or alive.

Mrs Connell was indeed an angel, she looked after her and little Georgie as if they were her own family.

Alice wrote to Father Brown at St Ann's and told him about the birth. He came and offered to accompany her to the hospital. She was allowed to see the baby, who they said was gaining weight. Alice could not believe her eyes - such a little doll, too small to dress, just wrapped in soft flannel.

The Doctor told her they had thought the child would not survive, it appeared that she was proving them all wrong. Father Brown asked Alice to name the little girl and he would baptise her so she was christened Florence Jenny, these being the names that George had chosen, always sure that the baby would be a girl.

So for four weeks Alice trudged backwards and forwards to the hospital to be with her child who was doing quite well and now weighed 5lbs. She was now allowed to take her home. Mrs Connell had knitted lots of tiny clothes and so she was dressed for the first time.

As she sat in her comfortable room, with baby Florence and Georgie in her arms Alice counted her blessings, but could not help shedding a few tears and wishing her dear George was there with them.

෬ Chapter 4 ෨

Alice was now stronger, in fact was looking rather well due to the care and kindness received from the Connell's. She decided it was time to look for work, so arranging for Mrs Connell to mind the children, she set off, not really knowing where to start. As she walked along the embankment a voice said, "Hallo Alice" and turning she saw walking beside her Tommy Kirk, a porter friend of George's from Covent Garden.

"How's life with you?" he asked. Alice told him what had happened since George's death.

"Poor little woman," he said kindly, "So what are you going to do now?"

She answered laughingly, "Survive or die in the attempt."

"Why don't you try up the market? Someone might find you something." Tommy said.

"That's a good idea, I'll do that," she replied.

Reaching Lambeth Bridge he said, "Goodbye Alice, best of luck."

She walked until she came to Maiden Lane reaching the spot where George's box once stood. Sadly staring at the pavement a thought entered her mind. Why not come up here and work, claim George's pitch and become a cartminder.

Turning she hurried home and telling Mrs Connell of her plans was told, "Don't be silly Alice they'll never let you do it. It's a man's job."

"I don't care" she replied, "I am going to start tomorrow morning." Opening the box that held George's personal belongings, she took out his cartminders badge, issued by the Covent Garden Association, allowing him to claim his pitch.

The next morning at 4 am she left the house and made her way to Maiden Lane, George's badge pinned to the lapel of her coat. She had no idea how or where to start, but spotting a horse and cart pulling into the kerb, approached the owner, "Good morning Sir," she said, "I'll take care of your produce and see it safely on to your cart when it arrives." He looked at her for some seconds, then roared with laughter.

"Christ!" he said, "A woman cartminder, what's the world coming to? You can't be serious?"

"Oh yes Sir," she replied, "I am Alice Brown, this was my husbands pitch and I am taking his place. He died, you see."

Realising who she was he put his hand on her shoulder and said, "I'm sorry, alright I'll give you one and six for three mornings, that's what I paid George."

Alice agreed, adding "In advance please Sir."

"Well we are business-like aren't we?" he said, "alright be sure and get the porters to load up properly and give my horse its feed at eight o'clock, I should be back by nine," and handing her the money he left to go into the market.

Over the next two hours the lane bustled with horses and carts, a few motor vehicles and barrows. News spread that George's widow had claimed his pitch. There was much laughter and ridicule, but most were kind and helped by giving her advice. The flower sellers, carrying their huge baskets were very friendly and warned her about some of the men, saying, "they'll try it on with you love, being so young and good looking," but Alice said "Let them, they'll get more than they bargained for," showing them her clenched fist.

So began Alice Brown's initiation into a man's world.

She found a wooden box and placed it against the railings opposite the little church. This gave her a feeling of security, also it was near the popular Rules Restaurant.

It was said that King Edward when he was Prince of Wales, liked to dine there, because of its famous gourmet dishes. Judging by the delicious smell that came from the kitchens, Alice felt sure that this was true.

The priests soon came to know her, she looked forward to their, "Good morning Alice, God bless you." The nuns from the convent would also stop and ask about the children and often gave her little gifts for them.

Winter had now come. She put many layers of clothing on for protection, but realised she would have to get some boots. Her feet were frozen and she was getting chilblains.

Dolly the flower seller asked her, "What size are you Alice?" The next day she produced a pair of shiny brown riding boots.

"Try these on love" she said. Alice went into a doorway and slipped off her little ankle-boots (the ones she got married in) and pulled on the soft leather pair that laced up to her knees. They were much too big but some thick socks would remedy that she thought. Going out she was inspected by Dolly.

Alice said "They'll do fine, how much do you want for them?"

"Nothing for you love, I had them given to me by a gent - Lord something or other."

"A Lord" said Alice, "Oh my, fancy me wearing something that belonged to a Lord."

It did not concern her that they were men's boots after all she was doing a man's job. So kissing Dolly she thanked her and said, "One day I'll make it up to you my dear, good friend."

Working in Covent Garden was no picnic, it was a hard life, as Alice soon discovered, but she was a determined and gutsy lady. She helped load vans, move horses and carts when porters barrows couldn't get by. Street-traders, shopkeepers, coster-mongers, and flower sellers all came to respect her. No one could put or take anything without her approval. Her vocabulary increased with many swear-words. She found this necessary as at times this was the only language they understood.

She developed a strong love of horses, and could handle even the most vicious of animals who only knew the whip as a command. Her pockets always held an apple or titbit for her favourites.

One day crossing Waterloo Bridge on her way home, a horse and cart passing suddenly stopped, the poor animal recognising her, mounted the pavement much to its owners anger, causing much confusion as the traffic was held up for some considerable time. It resulted in the poor beast getting a whipping.

Alice went home quite sad. Life was indeed hard when a little kindness causes such trouble.

She now had complete control of her life and was making a fair living, enabling her to pay Mrs Connell and keep her children well fed and clothed.

The outdoor life had given Alice a warm and rosy complexion. She was indeed a very striking looking woman - men often gave her a second glance, some asked to take her out, but she always refused.   She had been a widow for eighteen months, her heart still ached for George.

The only time she allowed herself to cry was when she visited his grave, always taking the best flowers she could get from Covent Garden flower market.

෬ Chapter 5 ๛

One morning a porter named Fred arrived in the lane with a barrow stacked with a customers order.

"Where's Stoller's van, darling?" he called to Alice; she ignored his question.

"Hi! Didn't you hear me?" he asked.

She turned to face him and said, "I do not answer to darling, not by you or anybody. My name is Alice."

"Hoity-toity Madam, I beg your pardon" he said, then bowing and raising his cap he asked, "Please Alice, where do I park my load?"

She directed him to a van just along the lane. After he had finished unloading his barrow he winked at her and said,

"Thank-you darling, I'll see you again," and laughingly walked off.

Dolly the flower-seller, observing what had happened said, "He's right you know Alice, you do get on your high horse from time to time, he meant no harm. In fact I think he fancies you. Don't shut yourself away, you are too young, live your life and enjoy it. God knows you work hard enough."

Alice blushed and made the excuse that she was wanted by a customer, and hurried to the other end of the lane.

That night she was very restless and could not sleep. Dolly's words repeating over and over in her mind. She felt sorry she had been so nasty to the porter Fred and resolved next time she saw him she would apologise for being so high handed.

As Christmas drew near, the beat policeman had warned her, "Keep your eyes open Alice, there are lots of thieves about, they'll pinch anything they can."

She thanked him and said she would do so. He had hardly left the lane when someone shouted, "Watch him Alice, he's just pinched something off Waller's van." She turned just in time to see a man running with a box on his shoulder towards Southampton Street. She ran after him shouting,

"Come back here, you thieving swine!"

But before she reached the end of the lane, she saw a man rush forward and knock him to the ground. He said, "It's alright darling, I've got him."

She recognised the man, it was the porter Fred. Someone shouted, "Give him a good hiding!" but another voice said, "No need for that." It was the policeman, who quickly took the rogue off to Bow Street.

Fred enquired, "Are you alright Alice?" she replied, "Yes" and thanked him for his help.

"Come and have a drink with me?" he asked. Not liking to refuse she said she would later. So when the lane had emptied and all her customers had gone, she accompanied him into the Bedford, a pub she had only seen from the outside.

He didn't ask her what she would like, but placed a glass of stout on the table in front of her saying, "Get that down you, it will do you good." She sipped the drink not liking it very much, thinking she would rather have had a port and lemon, but not wanting to upset him she drank it, then said "I must go now, thank you for the drink" and got up and left the pub.

She began walking home.

Fred was quick to follow, catching her up he asked, "Will you come out with me, to the Canterbury perhaps?" She said 'yes', she would go out with him, but not to the Canterbury, thinking she could not possibly go to the place, she had first met her dear George, not with another man. So she agreed to meet him at the Victoria Palace.

It was the first of many dates.

Their relationship developed, soon he was pressing her to marry him. He said he loved her and would look after her and the children. She had mixed feelings about it but convincing herself that she loved him, consented.

The next day she took him to Vauxhall to meet Father Brown, who was very pleased that she had met someone who would care for her and the children. It was arranged that he would perform the ceremony in three weeks time.

Fred lived in Spring Gardens off Wandsworth Road with his sister and her family. Next door there was an empty house. Fred applied to the owner and was given the tenancy. It was a little terraced two up, two down house, but was in a filthy condition, due to having been empty for many years.

Alice soon remedied this, she scrubbed and scoured until it was spotless. Fred whitewashed the ceilings, wallpapered the walls and painted the woodwork. He put new lino on the floors so with the second-hand furniture all cleaned and polished, it looked a little palace when they had finished.

The day arrived for the wedding, Fred wore his Territorial uniform and looked quite handsome. Alice dressed in navy-blue and white, as beautiful as ever. Georgie wore a sailor suit, and Florence looked a little angel in white, her black hair tied with pink satin ribbons.

Fred's sister and brother Tom came with their families. Mr and Mrs Connell and Alice's friend Dolly also arrived. Father Brown performed a short but sincere ceremony, Alice asked for the parable of the good Samaritan to be included, in honour of her dear friends the Connell's, to whom she was eternally grateful.

As she signed the register and realising she was no longer Alice Brown, but Alice Burman, she felt a slight apprehension. But Fred putting his arm around her and giving her a kiss, soon chased any doubt from her mind. Leaving the church they all went to Grosvenor Road, where Alice and Mrs Connell had prepared a cold buffet; there was plenty to eat and drink. Fred's relations making short work of both.

Alice was not impressed with the Burman's, they seemed a rowdy drunken lot, so was quite relieved when they all left. She wanted to help clear up the ravages of the party, but Mrs Connell insisted that she and Fred went home. It was arranged that the children would stay with her for the night, and Alice would collect them the next day.

Fred decided that Alice should give up her job in Covent Garden and that he would take her place. So life became much happier for her, she was able to take care of her own children. Soon she was pregnant, and on 16th March 1913, gave her husband his first child, a son, who was promptly named Frederick William, this being shortened to Freddy from the start.

Alice was surprised that Fred, apart from when the boy was first born, appeared to have little time to spare for his son. Life took on a very different meaning. He began to drink heavily, lying in bed and refusing to get up and go to the market.

Dolly came to see her and told of the complaints about Fred not appearing regularly. Customers produce was going missing, because he was spending more time in the pub. He was also keeping Alice short of money. So she decided then and there to do something about it.

Going next door to her sister-in-law she arranged for the children to be looked after in the mornings.

She waited for Fred to come home to inform him of her intentions, but he was so drunk she left him in the armchair to sleep it off. She explained to Georgia, who was now nearly six years old, that Aunt Sis would be coming tomorrow morning to look after him, Florence and Freddy until she came home from work. She lay beside him and held him close, he was such a comfort.

At 3.30 am she got up, left everything ready for the children and went off to Covent Garden. She was greeted with open arms, "Nice to see you back Alice, it's not been the same without you." Some wanted to discuss Fred's shortcomings and unreliability, but she would listen to none of it and said, "I am back, so forget it."

Reaching home at midday she was relieved to find the children had been well cared for. Fred was still in bed. On rising he spoke very little, he had no idea she had been to market. Waiting until he had eaten and had washed himself, she said, "I have been to the market this morning."

She was taken aback by his reaction. He just remarked, "Do as you like," turned and walked out of the house. She followed him and said, "Please Fred, come back, lets talk about it", he turned and very angrily said, "They don't like me up there, I hate it."

She put her arms around him and said, "Why didn't you tell me?" She held him close and felt sorry for him. So it was decided that she would carry on with the market and he would find a job elsewhere.

But work was hard to come by, lots of people were on the poverty line. There were strikes and marches. The suffragette movements were increasing. On Derby Day, Emily Davidson threw herself under the King's horse, sustaining fatal injuries. Mrs Pankhurst had been imprisoned after a bomb exploded in a house being built for Lloyd George. Alice felt their personal problems were trivial in comparison with other people's.

Fred's jobs were few and far between but Alice was content to carry the load. She made sure her children were well cared for. Georgie was now at school. Little Florence a lively child still undersized, but healthy, spent most of the time digging in the garden and making dirt castles, and Freddie, a quite happy baby, was not much trouble to anyone.

Apart from a relapse every so often. Fred stayed sober. So the year passed and when War was declared on August 4th, 1914, Alice was once again, pregnant. Fred was called up immediately as he was a territorial. He was drafted into the East Surrey Regiment. Alice was horrified when he appeared with full pack, complete with rifle. She hated guns, he was on embarkation leave for forty eight hours.

Georgie was delighted and ran out to tell his friends that his dad had a real gun and was going to fight the Germans. On Sunday night Alice said a tearful good-bye to Fred as he left to join his unit in Aldershot. She did not hear from him for some weeks, then a received a postcard from 'Somewhere in France', it just said, 'I am well, love Fred.'

There were dreadful stories being told of conditions in the trenches, Alice prayed that her Fred would be kept safe.

German warships had bombarded the Yorkshire coast and shelled Scarborough, killing some civilians. She wished she was not pregnant, the thought of bringing a little baby into such a dreadful world worried her. She carried on going to the market every morning, but as time went by there were very few customers. Most of the men had been called up or had enlisted, but she faithfully appeared, hoping to earn a shilling or two. Some days not taking a single penny she began to realise it was getting hopeless. Food was scarce, fruit and vegetables practically non-existent.

She got a job at the Savoy Hotel helping the Fish Chef for three hours in the evening. Wearing a loose fitting dress and apron to hide her pregnancy, she worked until a week before her baby was due.

She arranged for a woman to come in when the time came for her baby's arrival. Most nurses had been transferred to war work and did not attend confinements, only if absolutely necessary. Fortunately Alice's proved to be trouble free. She had a sweet little baby girl. Everyone remarked how like her mother she was, so it was only fitting that she was christened Alice Miriam. She had her mother's dark brown eyes and black hair, the other children loved her. Alice wrote to Fred and told him of his new daughter.

The war was taking its toll - Zeppelins were flying over London. Some bombs were dropped, Alice made the cupboard under the stairs into an air raid shelter. She and the children slept there every night.

In spite of the hardship, the sadness and horror of the war, life went on. It was two years before Fred came home on leave. He looked pale and thin, he had suffered some minor injuries, but compared with some felt extremely fortunate. Everyone was eager to hear about life in the trenches, but Alice asked him not to tell of his experiences in front of the children.

He had two weeks leave, spending most of it in the pub. He was not short of money, and spent it as if there was, no tomorrow. But the way the war was going, Alice thought that this could well be, so closed her eyes to his drunkenness, knowing what he had gone through. Time came for him to return to France. The whole family went to Waterloo Station to see him off. Trains were arriving with the wounded, there were terrible scenes of suffering. Alice was convinced she would never see Fred again, and held him close until the order came to board the train. She could not bear to watch it leave. Georgie said, "Come on Mum," and holding his little sister's hand guided the pram and his weeping mother out of the station. There was no news of Fred for some weeks. She was to see him twice more before the war ended on November llth, 1918.

Armistice was signed. There was much jubilation, crowds massed in the streets, the four years of horror, suffering and killing were over. Women waited patiently for husbands and sons to come back. It would have been better if many of them had not. Poor broken bodies, armless, legless, blind, deaf, shell shocked, demented, and gassed. There was no end to the heartache and despair.

Fred came through unscathed, Alice took the children to Waterloo to meet him, thankful to have him back. It was a happy little crowd that made their way back to Spring Gardens, Georgie bringing up the rear wearing Fred's forage cap.

They spent a week celebrating, Alice even indulged in a few stouts, for which she had attained a taste for. It took four weeks for Fred's demob papers to come through. He got all his back pay, but inspite of Alice's advice to save some, he squandered it away, mainly in the pub. Alice began to dread him coming home night after night aggressive and hopelessly drunk. He became difficult to live with. In his drunkenness he abused her verbally and physically, but when sober was always quiet and begged forgiveness, making promises he never kept.

The children were frightened of him.

Alice was at her wits end about what to do. He still wore his uniform which looked shabby and dirty. She pressed his civvy clothes hoping that he would wear them. He made no effort to find work, she was back up the market, which was slowly returning to normal. Fruit and vegetables were scarce, but the flower market was beginning to function well.

There were many poor people begging for money to buy food. The end of the war had not remedied this. Part of Alice's meagre earnings were often given to some poor wretch. The men who helped defeat our enemies were existing on charity. Little was being done to help them. Alice shed many a tear and prayed that God would. Seeing them made her realise that her own husband could not help being the drunken brute he had become. The hell he had been through was the cause. So with great patience and understanding she managed to straighten him out. He even got a job and life seemed normal once more.

The children were growing up, Georgie now a good looking twelve year old, the image of his dead father. He had inherited his kind caring personality and was the apple of his mother's eye. Florence, or 'Flo' as she had now become, was almost nine, she did not appear to resemble anyone Alice knew in the family. She was a real tomboy and was happiest playing rough games with the boys, she was the instigator of much mischief.

Freddie the youngest boy was so like his dad, a lovely child but a bit of a problem, he would wander off to the most unlikely places. His last little jaunt was most frightening, he was discovered sitting in the mud left by the tide on Albert Embankment. The Thames River Police spotted him digging for worms. He was quickly transported home, his father being advised to 'deal with him.'

Alice the youngest was a quiet little girl, very serious for her age. Still uncannily like her mother, she always cried when left with Aunt Sis.

Alice began to worry about this, realising that her children did not receive the care and attention she paid for. Her sister-in-law had become slovenly and neglectful. So she told Sis that she would find someone else, as it appeared that coping with the children was too much for her. Sis became aggressive and said, "You won't get anyone to look after them as I do."

Alice replied, "I hope not."

She began searching bill boards and shop windows, scanning the little adverts when one caught her eye.

War widow seeks employment as mother's help.

Apply Mrs Lawrence.

1, Spring Gardens.

Not able to believe her luck, Alice went quickly to see if this lady was suitable. Knocking on the door, she noticed the clean door step, which was quickly opened by a tall thin woman, who said, "Yes can I help you?"

Alice replied, "I do hope so, it's in reply to your advertisement."

She was ushered into a parlour which contained a green velvet couch and armchairs. The lace curtains were crisp and clean, and the table polished to perfection.

"I live opposite and I need someone to look after my four children in the mornings" she said.

Mrs Lawrence informed her that she had seen her and the children many times. Alice got straight to the point of how much she could afford to pay. They reached an amicable arrangement, Mrs Lawrence agreeing to get the children up in the mornings, give them their breakfast and take them to school. Alice had peace of mind once more.

But not for long, she soon discovered that she was pregnant and sighed, "Oh Lord, here we go again."

Confiding in her new found friend, was told not to worry things will turn out alright. She knew by rights she should give up work, but Fred had bouts of drinking and could not hold a job for long. No employer would stand for his unreliability.

Fortunately the pregnancy affected her very little, so she worked right up until the ninth month, arranging for Joss Purchase a man crippled during the war, who walked with two sticks, to cover for her while she was indisposed. He was a reliable man and only too glad to earn some money.

So on the 9th February, 1920 little Rose was born. Mrs Lawrence took complete control of the house and children. Fred kept out of the way and made no attempt to help. Alice was able to have plenty of rest. She was thankful to have found such a good friend and invited her to become the baby's Godmother. Mrs Lawrence was delighted. So the little girl was christened Rose Kathleen.

After two weeks Alice was ready to go back to the market. Fred still showed no interest in his family and had lapsed into a drunken layabout. Alice had to hide her money, which he often demanded, striking her if she refused.

Mrs Lawrence begged her to leave him, but Alice said "Where could I go with five children?"

So for three years she suffered at his hands, giving into his demands for fear of him hurting the children. Georgie was the one he picked on mostly, now fourteen years old, he often defended his mother against his stepfather's wrath.

Alice found him a job at a dyers and cleaners in Maiden Lane, owned by a very kind man she had known for years. Eventually he was given an apprenticeship and was offered a room over the shop. She made sure it was comfortable and well furnished before allowing him to accept. Although she was very upset about her son leaving home it was a relief. She saw him every day except Sunday. Each morning he would come down and kiss her, he was indeed a son to be proud of. His happy-go-lucky attitude made him very popular with the customers, he became a great asset to the business.

Life at home continued to be very difficult. When Fred could not get his own way, he would hit her or sexually abuse her. So once again, finding herself pregnant she went to see Father Brown. He was sympathetic but could only offer prayers to help her.

He said "After all Alice you married Fred for better or for worse, so go back home and try to make your peace with him and accept the child as a gift from God."

It was a very sad disillusioned Alice that returned to Spring Gardens. She went to her very dear friend, Kathleen Lawrence for comfort. As time went by and her confinement drew near, she arranged for Joss Purchase once more to carry on her work while she was away. She wearily trudged to market each morning. This was the worst pregnancy she had known, so when labour started she was very relieved, hoping it would soon be over.

Mrs Lawrence took the children to her house and sent for Grannie Wake, the midwife who was to attend Alice during the birth. She delivered a dear little girl, not unlike Freddie. The children were allowed to return to see their new little sister, they were delighted and said, "She's just like a doll", so the baby was named Dolly, not only because she was so small, but in memory of Alice's dear friend Dolly who had died many years ago.

The children went with Mrs Lawrence so that Alice could rest. Fred left the pub and staggered home.

Arriving at the house he yelled, "Where's everyone?" Getting no answer he lurched up the stairs, seeing Alice in bed he shouted, "Get up you lazy cow and get my dinner."

"Oh no," said Alice, "Look Fred I've had the baby," but he ignored her. Still shouting, "Get up! Get up!" he pulled the bedclothes off her. She picked up the sleeping child and managed to get across the room. He lunged forward knocking her through the open door and down the stairs baby in her arms.

Then reeling over he collapsed onto the bed in a drunken stupor, oblivious of the terrible thing he had done. His sister, next door, hearing screams came running.

She sent for the doctor who came immediately. Alice by this time was completely hysterical, so he gave her a sedative and Sis put her to bed in the children's room. The doctor informed the police that the baby was dead.

His report read:

'It appears the lady has fallen down stairs carrying her baby, resulting in the death of the child.'

Alice was quite ill for some time, unaware of the baby's funeral, or anything going on around her. Kathleen Lawrence looked after the children.

No one really knew the truth of what had really happened, Although Sis suspected it was Fred's fault, but kept silent.

Fred walked about very subdued, he accepted people's sympathy which came mostly in the way of a pint of beer. When her strength returned Alice confided in her friend Kathleen Lawrence that she was going to leave Fred. She was supported in her decision and Kathleen agreed to help her. They eventually found two clean furnished rooms at the Elephant and Castle with a school nearby for the children.

Back at Spring Gardens Alice began to pack their belongings. Fred walked in, he asked, "What are you doing?"

Alice answered, "I am leaving you."

He pleaded with her not to go, promising to change his ways. But Alice having heard it all before many times, ignored his plea's.

Facing him she said, "May God forgive you for what you have done, because I never will."

So gathering her children together, and with all their possessions packed on to the pram that should have held her dear baby, Alice and her little family left Spring Gardens to start a new life.

CB BO

•EPILOGUE•

Some years later, 1951 to be exact, Alice and Rose both received phone calls from Freddie asking them to meet him at Vauxhall that afternoon.

"It is very urgent," he said. Bewildered, but curious they both did as he asked. He kissed them and said, "Come with me and don't ask questions."

They walked along Wandsworth Road into a side street. Pushing open the door of a dingy little house, he took them up a filthy flight of stairs into a back-room. On an iron bedstead lay an old man, mumbling incoherently.

Rose said, "Oh God!" Whoever is he?"

Fred replied, "Our Father."

Alice turned ashen, Freddie fearing she was going to faint took her downstairs. Rose sat on the chair beside the bed, feeling uneasy as she watched two bugs crawling across the cover.

The old man opened his eyes and said, "Hallo Alice"

"I'm not Alice," she replied, "I'm Rosie."

It did not occur to her at the time that he thought she was Alice, her mother. He closed his eyes again and resumed his mumbling. She recognised, "Abide With Me," just that one line over and over again.

Holding his hand, her eyes streaming with tears, she quietly sang with him. Freddie returned with his sister Alice, between them they decided the old man could not stay in this terrible place. They found the doctor who had visited earlier, and asked for their father to be admitted to hospital.

He was taken to Lambeth Hospital and died that night.

The next day Freddie visited his mother and informed her of his father's death. She accepted the news and quietly asked, "Who's going to bury him?"

"George and I will," he replied. She went to a drawer and took out £25, handing it to him saying, "It's all I have, take it."

He did so, knowing it was useless to argue and refuse. He kissed her good-bye and was about to leave, when she said, "How did you know where he was?" He explained that someone who knew he was the old man's son had told him.

All five children attended the funeral at Wandsworth Cemetery and wept, not so much for the man, but for the terrible tragedy that had been part of their lives.

Among the flowers and wreaths was one that just said,

"Rest In Peace. Alice."

Alice was now 63 years old and still worked in Maiden Lane, no amount of persuasion by her children could encourage her to retire.

But at 74, as a result of an accident, which partly crippled her, she gave up, having been a cartminder for over 50 years.